NAVIGATION

poems by

Linda Elkin

Finishing Line Press
Georgetown, Kentucky

PANIC ROOM

NAVIGATION

ACKNOWLEDGMENTS

Grateful acknowledgements to the editors of the following publications in which these poems first appeared (sometimes in earlier versions or with different titles):

5 a.m. "My Father Returns to the 16th Century Before He Dies"
Antiphon: "Symphony," and "Rope"
The Bloomsbury Review: "The Feast"
Clementine Unbound: "Almost Enviable, Her Innocence," and "Simply Because He Is Mine"
Four Corners: "Traveling with My Father"
Green Mountains Review: "Words"
Kindled Terraces: American Writers in Greece:
  "Amorgos," "Ancient Game," "The Distance to Katapola," and "Donoussa"
Liberty Hill Poetry Review: "Acropolis Museum"
Midwest Quarterly: "Thanksgiving"
The Noe Valley Voice: "Story With No Words"
Peregrine: "The Canvas"
Poet Lore: "Gauguin's Model"
Southern Poetry Review: "Girl, Fourteen," and "Connecticut State Hospital, 1973"
Spillway: "Benevolence," and "Summer, No Wind"
Tar River Poetry: "Dancer"
Thema: "Scissors, Rock, Paper"
What Have You Lost?: "I Could Tell Him"
Willow Springs: "The Edge of Believing"

"Scissors, Rock, Paper" was nominated for a Pushcart Prize
"Simply Because He Is Mine" was the featured poem for the week of Sept. 18, 2018

Publisher: Leah Maines
Editor: Christen Kincaid
Cover Art: Adam Shaw, www.adamshawstudio.com
          Plunge, oil on canvas, 50x40
Author Photo: Andrea Scher
Cover Design: Leah Huete

Printed in the USA on acid-free paper.
Order online: www.finishinglinepress.com
          also available on amazon.com

Author inquiries and mail orders:
Finishing Line Press
P. O. Box 1626
Georgetown, Kentucky 40324
U. S. A.

Table of Contents

I have made myself a tribe
out of my true affections

—*Stanley Kunitz*

PART

ONE

Benevolence

The man and the woman
lie down in the hand of God.
Without them his fingers would stretch
from here to Rio and contain only grains of sand.
But God wants to hold the whole world,
so he starts small. Inside his palm
they slowly begin. Hand to hip,
tongue to breast, cock to violet undertow,
until at last God lets go and the ocean licks the stars.

Ancient Game

The women held on to the bull's horns
and jumped, legs suddenly skyward,
swinging their long bodies in a graceful arc
before landing on sure ground.

Over and over they practiced the familiar steps,
trained their sleek bodies to vault
over the earthly weight of the bull,
until their world spun upside down

feet brushing the course of the moon.
For a moment gravity released them:
they rode through the sky
as inviolable as gods.

Clasped hands around curved horns,
they grew accustomed to immaculate timing.
But just when they thought they had mastered
this exacting game of gymnastics, the bull tossed

his wild head and they became women again.
Their bodies in the blue air,
the heat of the brown-haired bull
rising up to meet them.

The Names of Girls

She is not what he expects.
He sees her every day
as she walks down the long hallway.

She is fourteen, does she know
her body is like the statues
of the great goddesses,

with their small breasts and strong thighs.
Know any man will have her, even if only
secretly. Know the power of being what he wants.

Because of her power he calls her witch.
She knows the names of girls:
Juliet, Persephone, Lolita.

He begins to offer her gifts,
books which she takes and returns.
He wants to change his life.

I am going to India, he says,
Will you come with me? My wife
has been my water, you could be my wine.

The girl is fourteen.
She wants to lie surrounded by red silk
and incense and let him drink her.

There is silence between them.
He is afraid she will say no.
He is afraid she will say yes.

Girl, Fourteen

Humming that we both hear.
Bees. I hold a candle. Beeswax.
You are old, in shadow.
I am in the center.

My red lips.

My mother-of-pearl earrings,
my throat lit golden by the candle I hold,
my bare arms. Bees.

Your anger, your face in shadow.
Your silence that makes the bees louder.

It will take years. I have time.

My red lips.

My eyes that look past your disapproval.
Your useless grip on me.

You sit sternly, in shadow. You are nothing.
My red lips. The bees outside,
the candle I hold upright.

I am all you have lost.

You don't speak. I have time.
We look in different directions.
My bare arms. My eyes that stare past you.

Whatever I tell you from now on will be
half covered with honey, half humming.

My red lips.

My lies.

Summer, No Wind

He watches me. I try not to notice.
Summer passes quickly now,
childhood is a blue dress
that no longer fits.

Nights I lie in bed and try
to recall everything that happened
during the day. Mama and Aunt Ellia sit together
and whisper. They look at me as if they know

some kind of secret. I used to be careless
like the boys. Never noticed my legs
as any different from my hands.
Mama frowns when I follow that man

to his door. She told me I was giving him ideas.
"What ideas?" I said. But I knew.
It's why he watches me. I want
to be little again, invisible.

The age when trees are your friends.
I am frightened of the purple sky,
the swimming snakes, the wooden totem
that never utters a sound. I want to go

where I can laugh out loud and follow
fishermen to the edge of the sea without fear
of being thrown into the water.
Without fear of being caught up in nets.

Gauguin's Model

My mother lived an ocean away.
My father was not a man who spoke to children.
I was not a child. That is what I told myself.
I was a woman and could do whatever I wanted.

I went to his studio three times a week.
Always at the same hour: three o'clock in the afternoon.
An easy time to disappear. He had the bed made
with white cotton sheets, the pillowcases

embroidered at the edges like my grandmother
used to do. I undressed behind a screen and slowly
walked over to lie down. If I did not remember my pose exactly,
he would correct me. Cross your ankles,

place both your hands near your face, palms down:
look at me. I felt proud when he told me how beautiful
I was. How no one else had such an amber glow to her skin,
such raven black hair, such sweetness

he could almost taste my innocence. It was when
he said those things that I knew I should not tell anyone.
I never fell asleep, though I could have easily napped
those still afternoons. I watched him as intently

as he watched me. Watched him move toward
and away from his canvas as if doing a slow dance.
His whole being absorbed with color and shape,
as if I did not exist.

I never saw the paintings until they were done.
Of course, he paid me. More than I could have earned
in any other way, so the money became secret too.
I longed to buy gifts for myself, wanted so many things.

Dresses. Bananas. Shoes with heels. Perfume.
Chocolate. Seamless nights. Secrecy. Sweet oranges.
Postage stamps. Boat fares. Coffee. Clean white sheets.
I began to notice how much everything cost.

The Embrace

*(after The Love Embrace of the Universe, the Earth (Mexico), Myself,
Diego and Señor Xolotl* by Frida Kahlo)

Diego, I was not dreaming of faces.
I was surrounded by planets, as you were.
Desert cactus, jade plants, pulled up
by the armful and held, roots dangling

from Her fingers like upside-down trees.
All of us suspended, no ground in sight.
The thought made me dizzy, so I held you
in my arms, a baby, but I could not bear your weight.

Her large arms encompassed us, strong as the earth.
A drop of milk fell from her breast.
We were a kind of family then,
roots, moon, cactus and a sleeping dog.

All the gates left open.
Each silence a waterway, an earthly channel
against doubt. The leaves all reached
upwards, single-pointed in their ascent,

as if straining towards the sun. I have reached
that way, when the sky hides all distance.
Did I tell you I was not afraid?
My dress was so red I could have been married in it.

Story with No Words

Let's say the girl is twelve,
wearing a one-piece suit,
black with tiny white stars on it.
The boy has a shy smile,
no hair on his face.
They stand with their toes at the edge,
arms overhead like arrows
and dive, splashing
at the same moment.

She recalls water down her sides
as she silvered under the blue.
Eyes open in another element.
And later, the sun shouting
yellow, yellow, yellow
to her dark shoulders
while a hand filled with blueberries
lifted towards her open mouth.

Years later when asked
why she liked this boy,
she can't think of a single word
they ever said to each other.

Words

We awoke in another country,
learned the language word by word.
Mostly offerings at first.

Tea. Music. Pillow. So simple then,
even when the words had more density.
Time. Love. Death. We learned

voraciously. The nouns
were the easiest. Hands. Eyes. Hair.
And the neighbors of verbs. Slowly. Quickly.

Soon even the simple words meant
something else. Toast was not food,
but hurry. Strawberries

not a meal but a whole morning.
Later, we possessed them by the armful,
passed them back and forth between us.

We talked for hours, yet language
was difficult. It led us to believe
in listening, then left us stranded.

The words began to thrive on their own.
Eventually, they failed us.
Go now. Don't go. The tea is cold.

Almost Enviable, Her Innocence

folding his shirts, stacking his underwear
into a neat pile, matching his clean socks.

A luxury, to trust him.
What he hid, he hid well,

in fear, or the familiar
childlike way one guards

the secret life. Was this the way
adults lie to each other,

seamlessly, without desire
to extricate themselves,

wanting only to be good,
to be loved, to be loved

without question.
Her husband's face

was a boy's face
when he slept, angelic,

and who has ever known
what angels think or do?

There must have been one thing
she never told him, she thinks now,

convicting herself for their ordinary failure.
Not now, not here, she'd say silently

when she woke. Or, perhaps,
one thing she never told herself.

Dreams buzzing in her head like mosquitoes
that she pushes away with her hand.

The Woman Upstairs

is afraid to fall asleep.
It is 2:00 a.m. If she lies

still for too long the mouse
might scurry across the mattress.

She is afraid the mouse will race
across her feet. He told her once

that he could break her toes.
Casually. Just a fact, he said,

not a threat. He had a silver
ring on his hand. She had kissed

those fingers once. The woman can't
see the clock on the wall but it is ticking,

keeping track. It is 4:00 a.m.
Black sky held in place by sharp stars.

The mouse might not come out tonight.
She might not hear his key clicking in the door.

The Edge of Believing

He would tell her, and she'd
believe him, that it was the cold

that made him act that way.
Late nights in their apartment

after the super had turned
off the heat, clouds of smoke streaming

out of his mouth, and it was the strain,
of pinching, of always having to squeeze.

And it was true, she thought, this morning
not enough for a cup of coffee,

a cinnamon doughnut, and the end
of the month coming up soon,

each day a candle blown out.
He said he was lucky,

she could count on that,
something would turn up,

and people always came back
once they'd seen his work.

And he was right, he could take an old
piece of anything, if it was wood,

and with paint remover, patience,
sandpaper, and his own mix of stains,

he'd transform it, make it a real find.
People would pay for his skill, his precision.

Then the rent would come, in cash,
and he'd promise, beg her to stay

another month, it was winter,
she was his one chance,

and she was still young, he'd say,
she'd have a thousand chances.

Spring was easy, he'd see to that,
a few dinners out, friends would come around.

Things would get better, stay better, and for a few weeks,
maybe months, he was right, wasn't he.

Then in summer it was the heat.
The heat, he said, was worse

than the cold, he could
hardly breathe in their apartment.

He would come home late, again,
once his face was cut, but it wasn't

his fault. He couldn't stand to see her cry,
things would change tomorrow.

It was the heat, he said,
that made him act that way.

The Connection

She says it was a coincidence, a bit of luck, miraculous, even,
almost as if clairvoyant. Her son was looking out

the window, or listening for familiar sounds,
the garage door opening, the car door slamming.

"Daddy's home!" he called out, gleefully, innocently.
How could he have guessed, not yet four,

the man who was Mommy's friend, the familiar visitor,
who was right now in the kitchen with her,

of course he didn't know. She was sitting
in a straight-backed chair, holding her breath.

The soon-to-be-lover was kneeling,
eyes closed, his head pressed against her chest.

Then, for the first time, they kissed. A surprise to her,
she says, that it even happened, so totally unexpected.

By the time her husband opened the front door, the guilty ones
were neatly standing, she tidying the kitchen, he stacking toys.

The boy, by then back to playing, didn't even look up once.
But now the son, too, is part of the story of the first kiss,

the wondrousness of it, of his not knowing,
yet calling out just the same to save her.

Blue with Sudden Orange

The blue of the bay matched exactly the blue
of the early sky, until mid-afternoon
washed over the even-hued beginning of our day.
The blue became deeper, heavier, as all the fish
swam in at once, six seals rose briefly
to the surface. A large boat drifted out of sight.
The light slowly shifted across the water,
the recurring seals, cloudless sky,
until the setting sun became the center
of the horizon. A small, circular glow
can utterly change the landscape.
The way sex takes up more space
than the space it actually happens in.

Waiting For Her To Cross Over

What he possesses is not patience, but willingness.
Orpheus in the corner with his lyre.
He knows how the body lives on both sides,
keeps his eyes open until the moment is so bright
he passes through. It was always like this:
light and then dark. A world revolves
around the axis of the next kiss, the one never taken.
When Eurydice gets close to him, so close
she will pass through from dark to light
on a single spark, she is pulled back by white silk.
The cloth is luminous and Orpheus solid as a dream
in the moment of awakening, caught in both worlds.

PART

TWO

God Hands Me a Knife

God hands me a knife.
Expecting what? For me to sever
memory and ability? To make
the air sing with one swift cut?
The task is to manage the knife,
balance its intractable weight.
I test its sharpness against my thumbnail,
and this one familiar gesture provides
me comfort, as if I'm back in the kitchen
more concerned with potatoes than time.
God is stubborn, doesn't care about
dividing life into past, present and future.
Thinks it's a foolish pastime, a trick we play
with language. God says it's all one.
But I know better: why else the knife?

Thanksgiving

Standing at the long wooden table, I lied.
I lied because I loved them and because
I wanted them to love me back.
When it was my turn, I said I was thankful
for the love of my family and friends.
It was what we all said, none of us looking
at the faces across the table.

That morning I had watched a stark gray flock
of birds arc in figure eights across the sky.
Leaden gray, ash gray, then suddenly the light
pierced through the fog and each wing,
each handsome muscled wing,
turned sapphire in the morning sky.
And all day I, too, was brushed by fire

and then denied it. All of us standing
at the table waiting to hear the polite
murmurs of thanks and praise, which I said,
which we all said, and really no one was lying.
Just leaving out praise for bright wings,
leaving out that sometimes it is only by the sudden
grace of sapphire that we are kept alive.

Scissors, Rock, Paper

I understood scissors
cut paper. Could hear them
opening and closing,
the sharp machinery of slicing.

Rock was easy to imagine:
a hand coming down hard,
a weapon in the hand,
the sudden crushing.

Earthquake, land-
slide. Terror lives
in rock. Easy to see
how rock wins.

Paper covers rock.
The least conceivable
threat. Nothing broken,
everything still intact.

I never understood
that to simply disappear from sight
was another way to lose.
We never called it violence.

Rope

As a child I learned
to tie a rope around my waist
so that when the quiet ones
were in danger, I would burn
with even the slightest tug.

I was summoned, silently,
by their delicate fingers tightening
around the coarse rope.
I could even tie it around my neck.
The little ones had such small hands.

Maze

The girl says *let's not make it easy this time,*
and puts the pieces down randomly.
Last time we played this game,
we planned straight, uncomplicated lines to travel.
She got from start to the diamond tiara
in one turn. I went from dragon to empress
in a cinch. The girl says *when it's easy,*
you can make a dilly-dally move.
Now it's a mess, all the pictures
we're striving for, blocked.
She says *when you can't get there,*
sometimes it's good to wait. She's waiting
until the landscape changes, and she has a plan.
We're both heading for the center of the labyrinth.
Most of our paths blocked, we move backwards,
in circles. I'm staring at the board, stuck.
The girl is only six and she's faster, she's better
at this than me. Tonight I've told myself:
Don't worry about money or work, don't think
about dating. Don't think about the future.
Just move your little blue marker until bedtime.
The girl is leaning forward, flushed with glee.
Go on Linda, your turn, it's a fun game.

End of Summer

The boy can't stop thinking of Godzilla.
When he goes to the beach,
as soon as he gets his feet wet,
Godzilla steps out of the ocean.
When he gets on a plane, the monster
sits next to him. He asks me
why I don't have children, he wants
another cousin. *It's late,*
I tell him, *I'm tired, I can't think.*
My head surrounded by a halo
of pain. Not his question,
but every question ignites
another mortal spark, that flares
and cools in the stern light.
It's 40 minutes past his bedtime
and we're playing cards. He refuses
to win because then the game
would be over, so he's playing
the wrong cards, purposefully,
then I begin to lose also,
both of us serious about not stopping,
staying up late, stealing time
in our trick to evade Godzilla.

The Austerity of Blood

When I
first heard
the news
my life
I knew
I would
give for
his life.

Elegy, 1969

Saturday nights were the safest
for runaways. No cop dared

to slam a kid in a crowd, a kid
expected home at night, whose parents

might be lawyers. Late that Saturday,
at the Fillmore East,

Janis Joplin said they'd sold
all the seats they were going to sell.

She wouldn't sing until they opened the doors
to let *the people in.*

Jimmy, Zak, Nelson, the rest of us, *the people.*
Mostly runaways. Mostly teenagers.

Tenement apartments, the tumble
of small change. Zak carried Janis

off the stage that night, back to her hotel,
too drunk to catch a cab. Too cold

to touch the iron banisters. Your fingers
would burn, the stairs, the sidewalk

wrapped in cracked ice. Jimmy told us
he'd had a dream that night:

we were dancing in a crowd,
all of us together, he could see our faces,

the music too loud for talking,
suddenly it was quiet, and he stood alone.

When we heard that Nelson was gone,
that he fell, that he'd fallen

off a roof that night,
time expanded, froze: click

the door shut, click he was gone.
We never said drugs, we said ice.

He was our angel, he must have been dancing,
he was our supple lion, who slipped.

Not just another kid who lost his balance
and fell onto filthy asphalt.

We summon our dead to contain them,
crack them open, so they seem to sing.

Nelson, mane of wild hair, brother of Jimmy,
born in Fresno, no last name, winter 1969.

Connecticut State Hospital, 1973

A long distance phone call, the police.
A hotel, an unpaid bill, a limousine, a hospital,
thorazine. The question of a car, how I'd get there, how soon.
A highway, an exit, a parking lot, a doorway.
Three nurses in a small room,
one with freckles who spoke to me first. *Sweet,* she said,
Cheri is the sweetest one on the ward.
A hallway, green linoleum that smelled
of urine and pine sol, and an old woman
with savage red lipstick, whispering
yes, yes, introduce him to me, my dears, but wait,
first let me touch-up my lipstick.
Cheri, face puffed and swollen,
not surprised to see me, glad I'd come.
Trust me, she said, *I'm getting married,*
I'll get my own house soon. The nurse said *yes,*
and a white dress, while a woman
with watery eyes called for her lost dog,
snapped her fingers.

I Could Tell Him

I used to live on the 18th floor
of an apartment building on the Lower East Side.
Spent a lot of time waiting
for the elevator to take me down.

What I liked best were buses and subways.
The Avenue D bus took me to school,
to Rachel's house, and all the way cross town.
The subway took me anywhere and fast.

My father is still up there, looking out
over the East River, watering his plants.
He wants me to tell him something I remember
that would prove his goodness.

I see his trees rooting in big pots
18 floors above the concrete
of Manhattan. I could tell him that
before he dies. Maybe he won't notice
he's not in the picture. I could tell him:

flowering white dogwood, willow,
geranium, basil. I could tell him
chili with black beans, gazpacho,
crusty Italian bread. Maybe he
won't notice he's not there.

The Distance to Katapola

I come from the other side of the island.
It may not seem so far away to you, he said,
as you have taken an airplane and a boat to get here.
But for me it is very far away.

There is a woman who once walked
from where we are standing to the house
I was born in. To walk there could take fourteen,
fifteen, sixteen hours, and you must walk

narrow goat paths on top of the mountains.
The walk to the other side of the island
is very close to the sky, he said.
Can you imagine, to walk from here to there?

It is so far away you might expect another language.
At times I long for my childhood home,
where I lived, as here, very close to the sea.
You have no idea how far it is

as you have taken an airplane and a boat
to arrive where we are standing.
But believe me, I was born in a different
part of the world.

I did not leave the other side of the island
until I was twenty-one, and now to return
is a journey I rarely make, and never in winter
when the seas are rough. I know of a woman

who walked the length of this island.
She walked farther than even the goats have gone.
How can I explain to you how far
I have traveled? If you were to see

the house I was born in, the long path
from the sea leading to that house,
what would you expect? Look at anything here:
this olive tree, that bright red fuschia,

the small yellow cat at your feet. You would see
each of these on the other side of the island
and you would say they are exactly the same.
You would say Dimitri must have forgotten

what it is like to be young. That the trees
must have looked different to him.
Tall trees with the arms of giants.
Dimitri must be saying that childhood

is the other side of the island, the place where
we grew up that is now so far away. Oh, but you
would be wrong. No, my friend, I am saying
where I come from is very far away.

Waiting for the Light

I stop on the corner of First Avenue
and Fifteenth Street to answer the voices.
Will you know what to do? Yes.
How will you know? I will trust myself.
Are you sure? Yes.
                              The questions
are that simple. I have no choices to consider.
This city which is consistently gray
and noisy is filling up with the pink
silence of cherry blossoms. It is April.
One more block and I will enter
the hospital where my father sleeps.
I stand still and wait for the light to change.

Traveling with My Father

Morphine, coma, eyes mostly closed
or open and believing anything. I poured
a thimble of watered down juice,
told him it was champagne, balanced
it on his parched lips. *Let's take a trip somewhere*, I said.
Pick a place you've loved. Europe, he decided.
My father held a New York City subway map, just in case
we got lost, while I wheeled his chair
down the dingy green hospice hallway
into the gold light of Florence.
Ponte Vecchio in late afternoon, stalls of jewelry,
not too crowded, we traveled
leisurely, almost hand in hand.

Then just as easily we were in Paris
sitting by a window, eating raspberry tarts.
Superb, my father said, nodding, satisfied.
Not once did he attack, did I flinch
or fight back. God of pain
and frailty. God of forgetfulness.
It took him losing his mind, then losing
his body bit by bit, for us to finally get here.

Not Far from the Beginning

My father died at seventy-seven
with no friends to mourn him.
When he was just fifteen
he went to City College
to study photography.
What are you, some kind of moron!
said his father. *What will you do,*
stand on a street corner and take pictures!
Every voice became his father's voice.
The subway screeched and roared
across the Williamsburg bridge,
back and forth between Brooklyn
and Manhattan. Back and forth,
father and son, on the iron track.
The awful machinery accelerated,
disappeared, and came back.

At the Edge

Rocks at the edge of the cove,
high tide and low tide,
sometimes seaweed, mussel shells.
The flat green stone I sat on.
Once, a tiny crab appeared
and was gone just as suddenly.
Behind the rocks, a sheer cliff,
ice flowers dangling over the side,
firmly rooted, immune to falling.
There was no storm. I was gone
for only a month. When I returned
the rocks—those enormous rocks—
had all changed places.

Simply Because He Is Mine

After my father fell
in the shower,
the meanness
slipped right out of him.

Now he surfaces
in a coma, repeats
a phrase, familiar,
but useless,

except it links me,
animal-like, daughter.
His hands and
feet, familiar, similar

to my own. His mouth
opens and closes.
I feed him fish and rice,
overcooked carrots,

hold the fork
to his mouth, then the cup,
the sweet, pale juice.
I watch him sleep, hold

his hand, claw-like,
the grip he has
no control over. My father,
on morphine, hours pass

before he opens his eyes.
I wait by his bed, watch him,
talk to him, while he sleeps.
Nothing between us but

the familiar form
of our bodies, needs
simplified. I coax him
to breathe, his one last job.

You are my flesh and blood,
he used to say. I sit
by my father, watch over
him, flesh of my

flesh, daughter, father.
When he wakes, I feed him,
simply because he is mine.
Simply because he is mine.

The Feast

A few hours after my father's death
I invited him to a meal in his honor,
and he lingered here on earth a while.

I prepared a platter of favorite foods:
Danish blue, Cambozola, and a curve
of moon-white goat cheese topped with raspberries
so bright they looked like they had tiny lights
inside. The bread was fresh and crusty,
I poured a cabernet he would have liked.

When he was alive he scorned the soul,
said there was absolutely nothing when the body died.

So how can I say that my father sat with me
a few hours after his death? How can I say
red geraniums were flowering and we shared
for one last time what only the body could love?

I welcomed my father into the house. What mattered
more than mourning that final night
was the table adorned, the elaborate feast,
the crusty bread, the fine red wine.

And he lingered here on earth a while.

My Father Returns to the Sixteenth Century Before He Dies

Today Michelangelo has painted
my father's hands. Something near
the ceiling must have called
to him, hovered
above him without sound.

My father reached up gracefully,
wrist leading, fingers falling
in a downward slope.
Just the way Michelangelo led us
to believe. The image lasting
long after the body has gone.

PART THREE

No Consolation

In Naples, once,
I bought a peach so large I held it in both hands,
turned its flesh toward my tongue

until I reached the rough pit in the center.
I filled myself with the weight of sweetness
until I could carry it with me everywhere,

like my hair, my eyes, my lungs.
That Naples does not exist anymore, *non esista più.*
Those men who sold worlds of peaches

from street-side carts are now too old to stand all day.
Their sons have moved on and the government
has cleaned up the filthy streets that only fruit

made fragrant. Now that my Naples is gone
it does no good to remember the fish.
Surely the aquarium where Paul Klee

framed his patient imagination
looking at opaque tanks the size of small paintings
is gone. I stepped off the bus at the last stop

and entered the ancient aquarium. The guards laughed,
asked what I could possibly want. *Che cosa vuole fare qua?*
No consolation in the deserted rooms

with dirty water and misshapen forms of no color
swimming aimlessly,
in this room where Klee conceived his fish. So I left.

A boy sat on a wall facing the sea
and threw empty bottles that sank quickly and modestly
as he cried out how he loved this city

and would never leave her. *La mia ragazza,*
my girl, the boy said as he gestured out to sea.
The boy is gone, the women

are distant relatives I never got to know.
Non conosco nessuno adesso a Nàpoli.
Not one familiar person now in Naples.

The trees continue to do their work, fruit ripens,
pesca, limone, uva, fico,
in a country full of strangers that have my face.

On My Sleep

(after Oskar Pastior)

It used to be that, when I went to sleep, sleep came.
Sometimes, while lying beside me, your steady breathing
ushered me into sleep. When one of us turned over,
sleep rippled, like a wave, as if sleep, itself, was the sea.
It used to be that, when sleep came, dreams came.
A brief stretch of floating, as if the sea were breathing beside me.
I could dive in and come up wearing a man's shirt,
faded blue cotton with mother-of-pearl buttons,
so silky on my skin it could have been real.
Then sleep gave me diagrams of continents, contents of old trunks,
branches of olive trees, silver and silver again.
It used to be that sleep, tireless seducer,
favored me with gifts, always surprises.
Now sleep has loosened its grip, tossed me ashore.

Left Behind

What was not said, not to each
other. But was known, touched,
true. What was a kindness
not to say. What kept us
from shame or anger or plain
confusion. Not what brought tears,
but what shoved us outside ourselves.
Hollowness lodged in the body,
a blank voice, a cloud dispersing water.
What made rain was each word
moving up through moist air,
until they gathered, then fell.
Wet our skin, soaked us.
What was said once, or ten
times. What we left
behind, not said. What we kept
to ourselves. What forced us
to kick off our shoes and swim.

Donoussa

Even in this dry season, leaves grow
out of my heart on long vines.
No one believes me, but I can see them changing color.
I try to remember grasshoppers and fireflies
to prove I was once a child.
By the end of August the vines are covered
with dust. This frightens me almost as much
as my longing. When I am alone
two swallows fly by my window at sunset.
One, and only much later, another.
The sky goes blank without them.
At night I think about boats, the small *Skopelitis*
which took me to Donoussa and did not come back
until the storm was over. I sat with the Greeks
and watched the horizon, understanding finally
why they pray for fair winds. In ancient Greece
the ships never sailed straight out
to sea, they stayed close enough to always see
at least the edge of land.
Love gave me an island to keep in sight.
I navigated my small boat towards its shore.
When I cut the vines from my heart,
the sea rushed in immediately.

Wings

Ornette Coleman playing *Sadness*.
Those first five notes. Two steps to climb upward,
then a hummingbird hovering, all breath,
his breath, that must have reached that note
so many times he knew exactly where he was,
and stayed there long enough
for me to follow him, still climbing,
the musical scale a ladder to Jesus
that we fall from.
                    Two notes all it takes
to sink lower than we started.
I pick the needle up from the old record,
place it back down on the spinning black circle
I believe in. Dear Ornette, if my body enters
the breath of your body, if music is as true as prayer,
will I learn how to rise on that one last note?
Birds begin their climb from a pathway
of crumbs. The colorless air around
my ankles is already sky for them.

The Invincibles

They have tried everything.
Barbed wire to keep out invasions,
the forward march of relentless music.

They have even tried neglect; horseshoes
rusting in an open field. Still, the colored
balloons keep appearing. Rising up

as round announcements
of another intention entirely. They watch
them disappear, thin white strings dangling

behind like smoke. They cannot lock
them out unless they refuse
to look up. The balloons could also burst.

Symphony

The great composers knew
how to open a world and just as surely
how to close it.

An expectant hint of melody
flies over low ground.
Bird, by leaf, by bark-covered branch,

stillness accented by sudden whir.
The final note holds on,
lingers before the lights come up.

How closely we listen, gladly lean
toward resolution. How unlike
the symphonies of friends.

We are awkward in our human endings.
Squawks in icy water, then silence.

Their Hands, Their Lips, Their Eyes

Standing beside the simple lamb
we notice the shepherd's hands, fingers licked clean
and fortunate by the animal's eager tongue.
The other hand raised toward
the blue dome flecked with patterns.
The intricate stars are gold.

Even standing under the splendor,
we know the story is mostly about suffering.
But this basilica was before all that,
the sky still full of innocent bleating.
A single line of red for the mouth.
Each woman's arms raised in the shape of a vase.
Their hands depicted holding
the unseen and dependable.

Let Beethoven Talk, Let Chopin

Standing at the barre, I followed the girl in front of me,
learned her legs and shoulders before her name.
Sliding my feet along the polished wood,
the floor became my speechless companion.
Toward the end of the hour, my teacher
stood facing me, told me to move
only when I absolutely had to. Sunlight slanted
across the room in little squares, I closed my eyes.
At first just a stirring, infinitesimal.
I lifted my arms only when I was certain,
my body voiced into life.
Such boldness to have Beethoven
unfolding silk scarves inside me,
head thrown back, wild and precise.

Dancer

When the ruined bones of her hips
could no longer glide her into the air,
she sat in the middle of a Persian carpet
and danced with the palms of her hands.

Lessons the Body Learns

for Margaret Beals

After we were informed that Bach's
Well Tempered Clavier was a strategy
of exercises meant to move the fingers
through all the major and the minor scales,

That our legs were surely the most
mundane collection of muscle
and bone, the workers of the body,
not the physical location of the flame-like soul,

She said *Lie down on your backs and try
to move mechanically.* We began to lift and lower,
bend and straighten, point and flex
to the practical notes of the piano.

But when we were quiet enough
what we found was heart everywhere,
even in the hips, the knees, the useful toes.

Acropolis Museum

I did not know how large
they were until I was standing
next to them. Marble figures
more moon than cold. The folds
of their tunics were familiar,
their strong arms no surprise.
What I had never seen before
was their faces of radiant kindness.
What would it be like
to live believing these ones
shared the world with you?
Bone into socket, socket into bone,
even death could be fitting.

Photograph, Scotland

A landscape of expansiveness.
Sky. Hills. Meadow. Two tall stones,
rough-textured, solid.

You watch them almost walking,
shapes across the meadow.
Lovers. Mother-and-Child.

You keep thinking, *the two of them*,
as you can't imagine such ancient stones
moving at all unless they are moving together.

The meadow is constant.
It is only these stones-which-are-not-stone
that braid in and out of time.

Amorgos

Just beyond the blue domed church, a marble
woman stands, hidden on an unmarked path.
She no longer has a head, arms or hands.
Even though her face is gone, She watches you.

At first I called her broken, incomplete.
Yet every day as I took my meals and swam
I knew She was standing there above me,
both of us so safe we could have been whole.

Red Necklace

What is the age when you start
counting backwards? Only five more
years till the wheels stop
their mad spinning, only ten,
only twenty? I would try
to be still in my heart
if it were not for the wild geese.
I just can't see myself sleeping
through the clamor. Something stirs
and I jump up to greet it. Leaves can't resist
the slightest wind. My red necklace
taps me lightly, where it falls
in the space between my breasts.

The Canvas

(after the painting *The Buddha* by Odilon Redon)

The sky is three shades of blue, with gold
speckled like stars, as if the color behind the sky
could shine through. Even the bare branches
of the tree are lit from within.
See how the robe of the Buddha
is a kind of patchwork that shows how the world is made
from small pieces. The hem is blue.
The two bodies in the painting
presented side by side, bare tree and long-robed Buddha.
The sky is brighter because of these branches,
because it has been interrupted
and does not exist alone. Like the body interrupted
by love becomes bright.
I think Redon wanted the tree realistic,
not dream-like. I think he considered for a long time
before he put those dark stems with leaves
right there in front, colored them black and green.
If what you thought at first were flowers
were weeds that would never bloom,
you would not have been wrong to bend down
and touch them, to take whatever scent they had to give.

Additional Acknowledgements

I want to thank the following for all they have added to my writing and my life. Judith Barrington, Margaret Beals, Clare Blotter, Mike Edwards, Marcia Falk, Larry Felson, Jack Gilbert, Linda Gregg, Jane Hirshfield, Michael Jones, Bill Mayer, Naomi Shihab Nye, Steve Orlen, Steven Rood, Pat Schneider, Jean Valentine, Eleanor Wilner, Soapstone and The Vermont Studio Center for time; Flight of the Mind, Everyone in The Writing Circles for Women; my family: Dolores Elkin, for infinite love, Joe Rubin, Jesse Elkin Rubin, Selena Elkin Rubin and Gregory Elkin; Finishing Line Press for believing in these poems and making this book; Barbara Kane for lifelong inspiration; Ingrid Tischer: the soul of wit; Alison Seevak for essential caring and connection; Kasey Jueds for sharing our writing worlds and deep friendship; and Joe Smith, for his encouragement, insight, editing, and ongoing presence.

Linda Elkin's poetry has been published in numerous publications, including *The Bloomsbury Review, Green Mountains Review, Midwest Quarterly, Southern Poetry Review, Tar River, 5AM, Antiphon*, and in other journals and anthologies, including *Kindled Terraces: American Writers in Greece* (Truman State University Press).

She earned an MFA from the Warren Wilson Program for Writers and was awarded writers residencies at Soapstone and the Vermont Studio Center. She taught creative writing workshops for 12 years in San Francisco.

Linda grew up in NYC and moved to San Francisco in 1978. She now lives in Oakland, California where she works as a Realtor.